Employee of The Year

Written By Eric Webster, Michael Todaro And Shanan Custer

Base Upon Original Concept by Michael Todaro and Eric Webster

© The Producing House 2012

Employee of the Year

The Evening:

OSHIOS (OH – SHE – OHS) Is a large multinational corporation with ties to many countries around the world and billions of dollars in profits. The exact product or service that OSHIOS provides is vague at best. In fact the company is so big and diluted that most employees are hard pressed to answer, "What is OSHIOS?" However they know what they do, but not what the big picture is. OSHIOS prefers it that way. Their yearly Employee of the Year party has been held in years past in Aspen, The French Riviera, Brazil and many other exotic and fancy locations. This year, primarily for legal reasons, they have decided to open up its year-end company party to include non-management types from all branches of their wide reaching corporation. Also for the first time, lower level employees will be considered for the coveted OSHIOS Employee of the Year award. They have decided to rent out "this" facility this year to make the event more "accessible" to all of the first time invitees.

The night includes dinner, (Dinner can be optional and is the "Non-dinner" version of the show is explained in the script), an awards show and hired entertainment in the form of a married Karaoke host couple. Awards include accomplishments in the past year at work, culminating in the vote for the "Employee of the Year" award!

However as the night progresses the management and non-management types clash in a battle of class warfare as the "99% ers" are desperately trying to fit in and fight for acceptance.

OSHIOS is a phonetic spelling of the word Otiose which means "Serving no practical purpose or result".

Quick character descriptions – more in depth bios of each character included at end of script

NON-MANAGEMENT

Lonnie Anderson-

Male 40 Plus. Warehouse manager from a local hub. Loud obnoxious but with a big heart. Means well. Ralph Kramden goes to a fancy party. Singing skills a plus, not necessary.

Ken Carrington -

Male 30 Plus. Sales. Recently let go from company. Shows up Drunk, Uninvited.

EMPLOYEE OF THE YEAR
WINNER TAKES ALL OFFICE PARTY SMACKDOWN
WWW.EMPLOYEEOFTHEYEAR.ORG

Sherman Allen -

Male 25 plus. Socially awkward I.T. Geek. Dance skills helpful, but not necessary.

Shay Van Porquet -

Male 20 plus. Works for Oshios in middle of nowhere branch in a made up european country. Weird accent. says inappropriate things by accident. Ridiculous flirt.

MANAGEMENT

Monica Monica –

Female 20 plus. Team Building leader / in charge of parties. Former Cheerleader. High energy.

Ed Bunker -

Male 40 plus. VP of Sales. Old and Crabby. Dance skills helpful, but not necessary.

Dee Dee Blue –

Female 30 plus. Human Resources. Hot, cougar type.

Gary Kzerltkzerkzon –

EMPLOYEE OF THE YEAR
A WINNER-TAKE-ALL OFFICE PARTY SMACKDOWN
WWW.EMPLOYEEOFTHEYEAR.ORG

Male 30 plus. Acquisitions Manager. Average guy. Very, VERY likeable. Super nice. Approachable.

OTHER CHARACHTERS - Irene Clara Ingebretson-Olson -

Female 40 plus. CEO of company. Socially awkward. Singing skills a plus.

Bob Clara Ingebretson-Olson –

Male 40 plus. CEO Husband Nice, charming, possibly somewhat effeminate, but not necessary. Singing skills a plus. Bob is from Germany. It is where Irene and Bob

Met.

Kelly Phobo –

Female 20 plus. Special assistant to CEO. . Prim, proper, conservative and organized. She is kind of a go between, between the two classes. She kind of lives on both sides of the fence. Singing skills a must.

Wanda Lamberton –

Female 25 plus. Karoake Host. Ability to look and sound like a fancy cheesy lounge singer and also look like a cartoon version of a rock and roll star. Singing skills and wide range a MUST.

Albert Lee Lamberton –

Male 25 plus. Karoake Host. Ability to look and sound like a fancy cheesy lounge singer and also look like a cartoon version of a rock and roll star. Singing skills and wide range a MUST.

Interns-

Various age and genders. Cast members who are interns at Oshios and will be taking on all the tasks needed to keep the show moving including picking up and counting EOTY Ballots. Also serve as understudies in the show. Each production can determine how many of these they need.

CONFLICTS TO KEEP EMPHASIZING THROUGHOUT SHOW Shay and Ed

Shay is flirting and dancing with women. He is engaged to Eds Daughter. As Shay Flirts throughout the evening Ed is constantly on him and angry with him, and watching him. Shay and Ed should emphasize this relationship and it's conflict in the "EOTY Video" that plays, making it clear there that Eds daughter is engaged to Shay and how that happened. (See Extended Bios)

Shay will sing a Karoake song that is a giant flirtation with every woman in the audience that will bring this conflict to a head.

Dee Dee and Sherman and Gary

Sherman loves Dee Dee. Dee Dee loves Gary. Dee Dee gets more and more forthright with Gary as shows goes on and she keeps drinking. Gary is married and a true blue guy, who is very awkward with this situation but very very nice about it. This conflict will all play out in an "on stage scene" during the awards part of program. They also will have a dancing "show down" in the karaoke segment. At the end Dee Dee chooses Sherman, and Gary is greatly relieved.

EMPLOYEE OF THE YEAR
WWW.EMPLOYEEOFTHEYEAR.ORG

Irene

Has a phobia of her employees, germs, and loosening up.

Bob

Bob has no real conflicts other than his happy attitude and great energy and his absolute enjoyment of everything tends to bewilder Irene. Bob should be dancing with patrons all night.

Kelly

She is torn between hanging out with non-management types, which she really is, or management types, which she is with most of the time. She is torn between both. However she spends the majority of the show tending to the needs of Irene.

Ken and Monica

Ken was fired and has shown up anyway to the event. He is drunk. He is ruining her event. It's her first event and she needs it to go well and he is single handedly ruining everything This will play out in the opening in an "on stage Scene" as Monica is welcoming everybody to the event and Ken shows up and comes on stage. Ken also sings a karaoke song that makes Monica uncomfortable. Monica should be following Ken around all night trying to keep him from doing horrible things, or cleaning up the messes he makes.

Lonnie

He is at odds with all upper management types. He is gregarious but slaps them on the back too hard and laughs too loud and eventually takes the karoake stage and sings "Take this job and shove it". This will be the song and the moment that everybody starts to get really heated at each other and at the end of this song is when the dance floor is divided and the "Fight" is about to start for real.

He defends and protects Shay and Ken and Sherman like they are his children. Lonnies feelings about management should be made subtle but very clear in the "EOTY Video" that plays.

These are the conflicts. Each conflict will have it's defining moment on stage or video so that every audience member understands the conflict and is aware of it. Table talk of these conflicts will re-enforce them, but each one will be clearly stated in a moment.

Employee of the Year PRE- SHOW

30 minutes prior to show start, patrons are let in to main room. They pick up their tickets and put on nametags. Monica makes sure that everybody has nametags and is checked in. She is accompanied by Kelly Phobo. Monica and Kelly will also be getting names of people to put on awards for later in the evening. Patrons should also be given designations for what are of OSHIOS they work for and titles.

Interns, Bob and Dee Dee will all be helping people get to their seats and welcoming patrons.

Characters filter into the main areas to mingle with patrons, discussing how they hope they are the employee of the year and start working the room for votes and establishing character. They let the patrons know they will be voting for Employee of the Year.

Door and seating

Monica Monica Dee Dee Blue Kelly Phobo Bob Clara

Ingebretson-Olson Interns

General table talk

Ed Bunker Shay Van Porquet Gary Kzerltkzerkzon
Sherman Allen Lonnie Anderson

Pre-recorded Music will be playing during pre-show.

TOP OF SHOW

There is one center stage. Behind the stage on screen is the Oshios Logo. At show time Monica Monica takes stage, gets people settled and welcomes groups and points out illuminaries among the crowd. Also informs them of bathrooms, smoking areas, turning off cell phones, and the format for the evening, I.E. when and how dinner works. This general information will differ from production to production and is to be written by each individual production. When these are done – she can begin regular script.

SCENE 1

MONICA:

EMPLOYEE OF THE YEAR
A WINNER TAKE ALL OFFICE PARTY SMACKDOWN
WWW.EMPLOYEEOFTHEYEAR.ORG

Well enough of that! HELLO EVERYBODY! And Welcome to Oshios's . . . 'sis Corporation Annual Employee of the Year Party! YAY!!! ARE YOU READY?!

GIVE ME AN O! GIVE ME AN S! GIVE ME AN H! GIVE ME AN .....E! Wait no....GIVE ME AN I! ....right?

(She turns around and looks at logo on screen)

GIVE ME AN I! GIVE ME AN O! GIVE ME AN S!

WHAT'S THAT SPELL?

Audience and Monica yell "OSHIOS"

Okay everybody! First off, according to Company Policy, we have to lay down the ground rules for the fun! Please welcome Human Resources Director Dee Dee Blue!

Music plays as Dee Dee takes stage

DEE DEE:

Hi everybody! Okay, so I need everybody to pay attention. *(reading from pamphlet)* Zero Tolerance for Inappropriate Touching. That's Z-TIT for short. (She laughs slightly) All employees are to be treated with respect and dignity. Inappropriate Touching of any kind will not to be tolerated under any circumstance. This includes sexual touching and other types of touching. Touching an Oshios employee, contractor, vendor or customer—touching may lead to a private discussion with me in the parking lot, or you may be asked to leave the party with me. In short: No Touching. (beat) And don't say anything about people who don't look like you. Thank you.

Music plays as she exits stage

Monica:

Notouching!

Ok so this is my first year putting this event together and I AM SUPER EXCITED. It's going to be GREAT! YAY! Now I know in the past we have held this event in

Aspen and London and Hawaii and the French Riviera and Branson and all sorts of really fun times. But this year we have decided to come here to beautiful (Insert city name). And we are so excited! We are here this year thanks to your little “Occupy Oshios” tent town in front of our main headquarters, and we are so...pleased to have so many non-management team members of OSHIOS with us for the first time! And of course we will be voting for our employee of the year throughout the evening, and also for the first time, we have non-management candidates! So a big yippee to all you 99% ers out there!!! Thanks for packing up your sleeping bags and cardboard lean-to’s and getting in that shower!!

The doors at the back of the room swing open. There is a lot of commotion. In comes Ken Carrington, he is disheveled and obviously drunk

EMPLOYEE OF THE YEAR
A WINNER-TAKE-ALL OFFICE PARTY SMACKDOWN
WWW.EMPLOYEEOFTHEYEAR.ORG

Ken:

HEY EVERYBODY! It’s time party like it’s....time to party!!!!

Ken works his way toward stage through crowd stopping occasionally and drunkenly commenting or talking to people. While he was working his way toward stage Monica is freaking out. Ken makes it on to the stage. Tries to kiss Monica, gives up and stands with his arm around her

Monica:

Hi Ken...Hey everybody it’s Ken Carrington. What are you doing here Ken?

Ken:

I'm here to win Employee of the year – THAT"S WHAT!! RIGHT PEOPLE!!

Monica:

But ...Ken....You were fired last month.

Ken:

Then why do I have this?

Ken takes out invite from his pocket and reads, slurred.

Congratulations Ken Carrington! That's me. You have been invited to the OSHIOS Employee of the Year Banquet and you have been chosen as one of the finalists for EMPLOYEE OF THE YEAR!!!

WWW.EMPLOYEEOFTHEYEAR.ORG

Monica:

Oh my God, this isn't happening. This isn't possible. WHO IS RESPONSIBLE FOR THIS?!?!?!

Ken:

Well it says right here at the bottom. Your's sincerely and yay you, Monica Monica Team Building Leader and Event Coordinator.

Monica:

WHA T?

Grabs paper

Ken:

See and it has about 20 smiley faces on it. That's you.

Monica:

Oh...Oh my God. I must have forgotten to take you off the list.

Ken:

Well I'm on it now baby! CARRINGTON IS ALIVE!!!

Monica:

Ok – I can handle this. Ken why don't you find a seat?

Ken:

You're a seat.

Awkward pause....

Monica:

What?

Ken:

I need to sit down

Ken leaves stage and finds seat. Monica collects herself

EMPLOYEE OF THE YEAR
A WINNER-TAKE-ALL OFFICE PARTY SMACKDOWN
WWW.EMPLOYEEOFTHEYEAR.ORG

and apologizes.

Monica:

Ok let's just move on -

And now, it gives me great pleasure to introduce you to you our Head Honcho, the Big Boss herself, here she is, your CEO Irene Clara Ingebretson-Olson!

SCENE 2

OSHIOS theme comes on, loud and powerful corporate music. Light go down. A single spotlight hit back of room on IRENE and BOB. OSHIOS theme plays. IRENE is dressed in a power suit and is all deer-in-the-headlights and can't see cuz of spotlight. and won't move until BOB gently pushes her forward IRENE andBOB make their way through the crowd. Once or twice IRENE risks shaking a hand or touching a shoulder and BOB immediately spritzes her with hand sanitizer. IRENE makes her way to the spotlight and microphone, stopping just as the music ends. Bob Sits on chair behind her on stage.

IRENE

Reading from card

Good evening! I hope everyone is having an enjoyable time. (flips card over, reads) I know I am.

The music starts again, the spotlight goes back and

we're at the beginning. BOB makeshis way back quickly to back of room alone this time while IRENE stands in the dark and waits. Bob walks up to stage again just like before except without Irene. OSHIOS themefinally ends.

IRENE

(holding note cards; KELLY will advance slides during PowerPoint)

Good evening! I hope everyone is having an enjoyable time. (flips card over, reads) I know I am.

It's always interesting to see people outside of the work place, isn't it? Everyone is so . . . different. And in sandals. That's fun. Some of you may think even I look a little different tonight. This is what I normally wear on Casual Fridays. So. And I'm here with my husband--

EMPLOYEE OF THE YEAR
A WINNER-TAKE-ALL OFFICE PARTY SMACKDOWN
WWW.EMPLOYEEOFTHEYEAR.ORG

BOB

I love you sweetie! YOU LOOK FABULOUS!

IRENE

Yes. (flips card) I want to thank Monica—

MONICA

Monica Monica! [Or: That's okay, you can call me by my first name!]

IRENE

(stares at MONICA) . . . – and my assistant Kelly for their work in making this (flips card over) special night possible. And another thanks to Kelly for going over my slides

one last time before this presentation. I've never had anyone look over my work . . . or touch my computer. So this is new for me. I am glad to be stretched in this way and

I embrace Learning Moments such as these. Thank you, Kelly. Speaking of

Learning moments, I represented Oshios at the Annual Core Directors Summit of Business Innovators and Leadership Professionals or as it's best known as: ACDSBILP [Ack-Duh- SS-Bilp].

SLIDE: Annual Core Directors Summit of Business Innovators and Leadership Professionals

At ACDSBILP [Ack-Duh-SS-Bilp] I learned many exciting Core Competencies that I would like to share with you. But don't worry, I know that this night is not about work,

but I think that what I have to share will be (flips through cards, looking) . . . fun. It should be fun. At ACDSBILP [Ack-Duh-SS-Bilp] I was an Ambassador for Oshios,

there to ponder the Wonder of Possibility. And my Wonder is a Possibility Rooted in Reality, but Reaching for Heights Unknown. One thing that I learned at

ACDSBILP

[Ack-Duh-SS-Bilp] is that while Reaching for Heights Unknown we can become nervous and not as productive or under-efficient. For example, I have come to understand

through the many fine coaches at ACDSBILP [Ack-Duh-SS-Bilp] that people accept the Unknown better if they are viewing something they find pleasant for approximately 5

seconds.

CLIP: Kitten

IRENE, cont.

Isn't that interesting?

With that said, I want to just quickly announce that there will be some changes coming to

the Oshios Health Plan, but it's really no big deal.

SLIDE: No big deal

And while change can be frightening, I think I'm at liberty to say that there will be some pretty great perks with this new plan.

SLIDE: Free Keychains!

But again, change happens.

EMPLOYEE OF THE YEAR
OFFICE PARTY SMACKDOWN
WWW.EMPLOYEEOFTHEYEAR.OR

*CLIP: kittens(IRENE counts slowly to 5)*Okay. Kittens. It's no big deal. Next slide, please.

SLIDE: Agenda Introduction Challenges Mission Team Action Item Wrap-up Q&A

As I mentioned, this was an exciting summit that really challenged me to think of new and innovative ways to incorporate Oshios's Core Strategies into our Strategic Model Plan that will eventually interface with both our Emerging Markets and our ability to create an Integrated Solution that will allo us—as a Team —to define ourselves as a relevant and Fast-Growth Organization that is committed to delivering our Mission-Critical Objectives in a very diverse and non-legally binding way.

KELLY SLIDE:There will be no promotions this year.

SLIDE:

Agenda Introduction Challenges Mission Team Action Item Wrap-up Q&A

IRENE looks back and KELLY gives a thumbs-up.

Through this acceleration of high maturity behaviors we will move beyond the stop-gap. Win-win. Basically, it's solutioneering at its finest. (looks at notes)

KELLY SLIDE:"Solutioneering" is not a real word.

SLIDE: Agenda Introduction Challenges Mission Team Action Item Wrap-up Q&A

But what does that really mean for all of you, besides the obvious? I really want us all to

be on the same page. There are no stupid questions.

IRENE gets a sip of water

KELLY SLIDE:This is a lie. If I had a nickel for every time one of you cubicle monkeys asked a stupid question, I would have a sh@!load of nickels.

SLIDE:

Agenda Introduction Challenges Mission Team Action Item Wrap-up Q&A

EMPLOYEE OF THE YEAR
WWW.EMPLOYEEOFTHEYEAR.ORG

I think it means essentially that we are committed—as a Team—to Integrating our Core Competencies into a System Development Program that will meet our Phase 1

Deliverables and in order to do that we must incentivize the workforce with monetary rewards.

Put another way:

SLIDE: Graph

You are represented by the red line.

But what is Oshios? What is it that we do exactly?

KEN:

(yells from bar, or with drink in hand) NOBODY KNOWS! Seriously! Ask any of these people, nobody has any idea what they do!

IRENE:

(stares at him for a beat) Kitten.

CLIP: Kitten

IRENE counts to 5.

KEN

I am now calm and placated.

IRENE

What we do is simple: we are committed to working on projects and agreements that will create mutually beneficial opportunities.

SLIDE:Oshios= Work + Projects/Agreements = Mutually Beneficial Opportunities=Oshios

IRENE

So this is what I would like to leave you with tonight: a thought really . . . about who you are and how you work and how you feel--

KELLY SLIDE:Nobody wants to know how you feel. Seriously.

EMPLOYEE OF THE YEAR

IRENE

--and how it matters little what we want to accomplish.

IRENE looks back. KELLY mouths "You're doing great!"

SLIDE:Oshios= Work + Projects/Agreements = Mutually Beneficial Opportunities=Oshios

I like to call it my Theory of Non-Hostile Acquisition in which I am the Key Enabler to the Systems that we—as a Team--create.

KELLY SLIDE"Team" is a metaphor. You have absolutely no control whatsoever. So drink up.

SLIDE:Oshios= Work + Projects/Agreements = Mutually Beneficial Opportunities=Oshios

EMPLOYEE OF THE YEAR
A WINNER-TAKE-ALL OFFICE PARTY SMACKDOWN
WWW.EMPLOYEEOFTHEYEAR.ORG

These Systems will allow all of you to leave behind the under-competencies and imperfections that make you inefficient and less desirable to the larger Core . . .the

Collective, if you will.

KELLY SLIDEThis is not a metaphor. You should be a little freaked out right now.

Because we can be perfect, we can integrate our strengths into the larger whole or

Assimilate them into a unit of pure functionability.

KELLY SLIDEFunctionability is also not a real word.

For all of you “visual learners” out there.

KELLY SLIDE“Visual Learner” is nicer than saying “idiot”.

IRENE turns to screen.

SLIDE:A graph of all of the departments and a really tiny dot with an arrow pointing to “You”

MONICA

(At table)

I see me!

IRENE

It’s my goal to do away with those troublesome concepts like “creativity” and “questioning” and “energy” and “ideas”—these trendy buzz-words will only serve to weaken the Collective. Because in the end the more you bring to the table the less

worthwhile you become to the Collective.

KELLY SLIDE: Resistance is Futile.

SHERMAN

(from audience) Holy crap! [Or: Really?!]

SLIDE:A graph of all of the departments and a really tiny dot with an arrow pointing to “You”

Yes, it is exciting! The reality is that you may have your job and you may your 401K but by 2016 the average cost of tuition at a private college will be about $250,000. Perhaps

it would be best to help them with their athletic skills or urge them toward some sort of trade.

KELLY SLIDETeach your kids to weld.

But tonight is about Possibility! Stay rooted, but keep reaching for Heights Unknown. The Wonder of Possibility is yours for the taking! Thank you for your attention. I hope this evening is (flips card over) enjoyable.

SLIDE:Enjoy Yourself at this Work-Related Function!

OSHIOS theme plays again as she exits stage. Oshios logo comes up on screen on fire

EMPLOYEE OF THE YEAR
A WINNER TAKES ALL OFFICE PARTY SMACKDOWN
WWW.EMPLOYEEOFTHEYEAR.ORG

SCENE 3

MONICA MONICA:

YAY!!! That was so super informative and well thought out. And so much to look at! Super pretty.

Let's here it for Mrs. Ingebretson-olsons awesome, super amazing personal assistant Kelly Phobo!

KELLY:

*(She and Bob have not quite left stage – she comes to mic)*All Graduates from Smith *summa cum laude* with a degree in the Romantic Languages and a minor in Women's Studies Can I get a what what?

Bob:

What what!

Monica:

OK everybody as you know the Employee of the year award is coming up. On each of your tables you will find a ballot. You can fill them out anytime, whenever you have made your decision on who should be employee of the year. To help you out – let's meet the candidates! Roll Film!

(on screen behind Monica comes short film about candidates)

Canidates film notes -Should be kept to under 3 minutes – 2 would be even better. -each candidates name and title comes up on screen with narrator VO, with footage of candidate working. -each candidate should have a ten to 15 second video diary segment to explain why they should win employee of the year. -there should be footage of them at work. -VO should include each candidates accomplishments during the year. **NOTE – GARY'S VIDEO SHOULD HAVE A LOT OF PEOPLE MISPROUNOUNCING HIS NAME TO SET UP A JOKE COMING LATER**

EXAMPLE:

WWW.EMPLOYEEOFTHEYEAR.ORG

V .O.:

Dee Dee Blue, Director of human resources

Video of Dee Dee at work is playing while her name and title appear on screen at same time VO is read. Dramatic music is playing.Cut to video of Dee Dee explaining why she should win employee of the year Cut to more video of Dee Dee at work

V .O.:

Dee Dee Blue has been with OSHIOS for 9 years. In the past year she has handed out over 3000 demerits for dress code violations. She also increased one on one interaction with employees by a whopping 44 percent. Her level of dedication seems endless as Dee Dee is frequently seen leaving work late in the evening.

*(Shot of Dee Dee Getting out of car in parking lot and walking to her another car and getting in, both cars drive off)*Dee Dee Blue, Director of Human resources.

-The content and script of the video can be determined by the director and each individual production. -Understudies will have to have there clips pre-made and the film will have to be edited each time an understudy goes in on a night. With the clips for each actor pre-made this is a relatively simple edit.

SCENE 4A – With dinner included

IF PRODUCTION IS NOT SERVING DINNER SKIP DIRECTLY TO SCENE 4B

EMPLOYEE OF THE YEAR

Monica:

Well we have so much more to come. Karoake is on the way people so don't forget to fill out your song requests.

We are going to start dinner here in just a minute and then after dinner we will be getting to our Oshios Awards for the past year, including, of course, our EMPLOYEE OF THE YEAR! YAY!

(Monica needs to explain how dinner will work here. This will vary from production to production)

Now before we start dinner, it is my pleasure to introduce to you our entertainment for the evening. Did you know that Karaoke is Japanese word that is a portmanteau of the Japanese word kara meaning "empty", and o□kesutora meaning"orchestra"? Isn't that weird? Japanese.

WWW.EMPLOYEEOFTHEYEAR.ORG

Anyway she has come all the way from *(Insert local joke, local small town)* , So she's super fresh! Ladies and Gentleman the karaoke stylings of Wanda Lamberton!!!!

Wanda takes stage

W ANDA:

Wanda and Albert Lee are dressed well and take stage.

Good evening everybody.

WANDA and ALBERT LEE will have a number of songs

ready to perform. These songs are "standards" I.E. "At Last" or "I've got the world on a string". Music to eat dinner by.

*This dinner segment of the show is app. 20 minutes long. As dinner is concluding Monica takes the stage***SCENE 4BMonica:**

Karoake is on the way people so don't forget to fill out your song requests.

Now it's time for our Oshios Employee Awards!!! Presenting our awards is the Director of Human Resources Dee Dee Blue and our Acquisitions Manager Gary Kzerltkzerkzon!!!!

(She pronounces name Kajagoogoo)

Music plays as they take stage – Gary is up on stage quickly and confronts Monica

GARY:

OK THAT'S IT – IT'S PRONOUNCED KA –SHIT – SER – SON! KA – SHIT – SER – SON! OK? EVERYBODY GOT THAT? IS THAT SO HARD?

There is a long beat....

LONNIE:

(From audience)

SHITSY!

EMPLOYEE OF THE YEAR
A WINNER TAKE-ALL OFFICE PARTY SMACKDOWN
WWW.EMPLOYEEOFTHEYEAR.ORG

Dee Dee has been drinking and has loosened up QUITE a bit. As her and Gary host this segment, Dee Dee is constantly touching Gary and flirting with him and saying inappropriate things. Gary is very uncomfortable and awkward. These moments are NOT in the script, they need to happen throughout this scene and frequently.

DEE DEE:

Thank you! How is everybody?

Okay let's get on to our Employee Awards! Gary *(She says name correctly)* Ka –Shit- ser – son - why don't you announce the first award?

GARY:

Well thank you. Thank you so much for doing that right. That means a lot.

DEE DEE:

You're cute Gary!

GARY:

Okay let's see the next award is the Supersaver Award, for Best Idea for Saving the Office Money. And this year for his idea for combining the CEO assistant with Office Supply Manager position - our award goes to: ____________(Patron's *name - male)*

Music plays as they take stage.

GARY:

Interviews winner

GARY:

Let's here it for __________ !

PATRON leaves stage.

Music plays as they leave stage

DEE DEE:

Next up is our Outstanding Newcomer of the Year Award! Awarded to the

EMPLOYEE OF THE YEAR
A WINNER-TAKE-ALL OFFICE PARTY SMACKDOWN
WWW.EMPLOYEEOFTHEYEAR.ORG

employee who is newest and best! This year our winner is I.T. Lead Sherman Allen!

Picture of SHERWIN comes up on screen. SHERWIN makes his way toward stage.Sherwin gets on stage and cannot take his eyes off Dee Dee. Dee Dee is CRAWLING all over Gary, and it is making Sherwin angry.

Sherman: Thank you everybody for this award...

Glancing back at Dee Dee Molesting Gary behind them

I am very honored to....

Glances back

I would like to let you all know that ....

Glances back

OK THAT"S IT. Dee Dee – I love you. And I challenge you sir to a duel!!!!!

Points at Gary

DEE DEE:

What? Oh this is sooooo hot.

Gary:

What? No – I'm not...She and I aren't....I'm married.

Sherwin: You are afraid of me are you?

Gary:

No it's just...I don't know what's going on.

SHERWIN:

JUSTIN BEIBER

GARY:

What?

SHERWIN:

Your Computer password is Justin Beiber. Anybody else?

He turns and kisses Dee Dees Hand

My lady

He walks off, triumphant... and trips slightly.

Music plays as he exits.

GARY:

Composes himself

Our final award is for Lifetime Achievement.

Lonnie comes running on stage

And our winner is: ____________(Patro'ns *name).*

Lonnie stands on stage bewildered PATRON comes up on stage.

EMPLOYEE OF THE YEAR
A WINNER-TAKE-ALL OFFICE PARTY SMACKDOWN
WWW.EMPLOYEEOFTHEYEAR.ORG

DEE DEE:

My goodness how long have you been with the company now?

General interview with confused patron.

Lonnie approaches Gary and Dee Dee after Patron leaves.

Lonnie:

So that is who is winning the lifetime achievement award huh?

Lonnie laughs really loud, slaps Gary on the back super hard

WOW I guess they are super deserving of that

Lonnie laughs really loud, slaps Gary on the back super hard

Cuz it's not like I've busted my ass for 20 years in the warehouse and have never gotten a raise or promotion, hell I would have settled for a lousy award

Lonnie laughs really loud, slaps Gary on the back super hard

But I guess not. That's just great. REALLY REALLY GREAT!

Lonnie laughs really loud, slaps Gary on the back super hard

Thank you so much OSHIOS

Lonnie laughs really loud, slaps Gary on the back super hard

Lonnie leaves stage controlling his anger

DEE DEE:

WWW.EMPLOYEEOFTHEYEAR.ORG

And that's our Oshios awards!

Music plays as they exit – Gary is obviously injured and Dee Dee helps him.

Monica takes stage

MONICA:

Well that was super fun!!! OK now coming up it's time we all shake our booty...

KEN:

W AIT!

Ken stumbles forward and takes stage

We have one more award, I want to give an award for Ethics.

EMPLOYEE OF THE YEAR
A WINNER TAKE-ALL OFFICE PARTY SMACKDOWN
WWW.EMPLOYEEOFTHEYEAR.ORG

Ken:

This award goes to a person who has been such a good little whistle blower. A person whose nosiness and tattle telling and endless report filling outing cost me my job. This years big jerk award goes to...

Monica runs and grabs mic and hands Ken a drink. Ken is distracted by the drink and wanders off...

MONICA:

OK! Thank you so much Ken.

SCENE 5

Monica:

And now ladies and Gentleman – it's time to party. Please welcome back Wanda and Albert Lee Lamberton!

Wanda and Albert Lee come out – change of costume – they are now in more "comfortable" Rock and Roll type garb. Music starts – LOUD – Lights go down – Party dance lights up full. It should feel like the opening to a rock concert.

W ANDA:

ARE YOU READY TO KAROAKE!?!?!?!

The basic format of the Karaoke / Dance Segment:

After each song is done, Wanda will invite up the next karaoke singerAny of the songs in this segment can be changed to suit individual production.

IMPORTANT: The intent is to get as many Patrons up and dancing as possible, but there will be patrons who do not. Designate characters to be table talking with the patrons who are not participating in the dancing. Irene is great for this. However, encouraging people to dance should never stop and the energy of this segment has got to be "through the roof". No character should stop. If they absolutely cannot get anybody up to dance then the dance floor should be full of characters. The dance floor should never be empty.

Song one - Wanda - Anyway you want it -Journey

Song two – Shay sings I touch myself - Devinals

Shay will work the woman on the dance floor on wireless mic with this song, also inviting women on stage for the end of song. Ed is on stage the whole time fuming. When song ends Ed grabs microphone.

Ed:

You are engaged to my daughter, and I'm going to Kill you you third world nymphomaniac!

Ed Chases Shay off stage. For the rest of the evening Shay is running from Ed, they pop in and out of the room. In general the two need to make frequent "chase scenes" back into the room and out. Each time escalating the scene. I.E. with various weapons, Shays clothes ripped, etc...

EMPLOYEE OF THE YEAR

UPDATE ON VOTING

Wanda:

Hey everybody it's time for an update on how the Employee of the year voting is coming Intern comes on to stage. Interns are gathering the ballots from tables and they are tabulating results backstage

Intern:

With_______% of the tables reporting, ____________is

leading by___________%. If you haven't filled out your ballots yet please do!

Song Three – Patron

Song four – Paton

Song Five - Ken sings tequila

The bit here of course is that the only words to this song are "Tequila". Ken however is slightly late each time it's his turn to sing. He stands waiting the whole song just to say "Tequila" and is late every time followed by and expletive. Production can determine the extent of the expletive and what is appropriate.

"Tequila....DAMMIT" Monica is mortified, near or on stage. She is begging him to stop the whole song.

EMPLOYEE OF THE YEAR WWW.EMPLOYEEOFTHEYEAR.ORG

UPDATE ON VOTING 2

Wanda:

Hey everybody it's time for an update on how the Employee of the year voting

is coming Intern comes on to stage. Interns are gathering the ballots from tables and they are tabulating results backstage

Intern:

With_______% of the tables reporting, ___________is leading by___________%. If you haven't filled out your ballots yet please do! THIS IS LAST CALL FOR BALLOTS.

Song Six – Patron

Song Seven – Patron

Song Eight - Sherman sings She blinded me with Science

Sherman will dedicate this to Dee Dee. Dee Dee is on dance floor with Gary. Gary is trying to escape her clutches still. Sherman will move to dance floor with wireless mic and through body language challenge Gary to some sort of "dance off" duel. Gary, having had enough accepts and the two of them exchange bizarre dance moves at each other throughout song, and exchanging the microphone and singing when needed. Dee Dee is impressed. This works best if the two actors are actually good dancers and this becomes a "Jets vs. Sharks" moment with the two of them with impressive dance moves. However it can also be done ridiculously, with really inane dance moves.

EMPLOYEE OF THE YEAR

Song Nine - Kelly Phobo – Sings Bad Romance

Kelly who is conservatively dressed and a little uptight sings bad romance. BUT DOESN"T LET LOOSE. She can sing INCREDIBLY but she should just stand there, with clipboard and glasses and belt this out. Stoic performance.

Song Ten– Wanda – Ballroom Blitz

Song Eleven – Lonnie sings take this job and shove it

This is the song that starts to bring the conflict over the edge. The non- management types begin singing along, and singing at management types. As the song goes on all characters should move to dance floor. It escalates into screaming and pointing fingers. The dance floor becomes literally divided. Characters will move patrons to one side of the dance floor or the other my persuading them to be on "Their" side. Eventually the dance floor should have a divide right down the middle from center stage. Lonnie, on stage singing the song, is now center stage and lined up with the divide on the dance floor. Tempers flaring, people screaming back and forth, and finally someone pushes someone. Lonnie yells "that's it!" drops microphone and dives into crowd. He however just hits the floor and lays there motionless. Everybody stares for a second at Lonnie on the floor and then they attack each other. This lasts for about 2 seconds before Kelly Phobo takes the stage and grabs the mic.

Kelly:

STOP IT!! EVERYBODY STOP! WHAT ARE YOU DOING?

The hub bub subsides and everybody stops the fighting, looks up at Kelly.

Why... are you doing this? Why? Isn't the universe big enough... for both of us? What is wrong with you people? We could work together. Why be enemies?

Because we're different? Is that why?

Think of the things that we could do. Think how strong we would be. Management... and non-management... Together. There is nothing that we could not accomplish. Think about it. Think about it. Why destroy... when you can create? We can have it all, or we can smash it all. Why can't we... work out our differences? Why can't we... work things out? why can't we all just... get along?

Ed:

Nicholson – Mars Attacks?

Kelly:

Yeah well it seemed to fit

EMPLOYEE OF THE YEAR

There is a moment of silence, a beat, then everybody hugs. Ed and Shay shake hands and make up. Dee Dee Shakes Gary's hand and grabs Sherman and Kisses him hard. Ken runs to Monica and to shake her hand, she grabs him and kisses him. Everybody starts to move back to the "Dance floor divide" positions revealing that Lonnie is still on the floor, face down, and has been this whole time. Kelly sees him, jumps off stage and takes care of him, waking him or dragging him off. While Kelly jumps down to take care of Lonnie, Irene and Bob appear as if out of nowhere. They have not been privy to the near fight. She looks out and sees the hugging and making out. Irene is on Mic.

SCENE 6

IRENE:

Well you all seem to be getting along well. And now Ladies and Gentleman it's the time we have all been waiting for – I have in my hand the final tally of the votes for EMPLOYEE OF THE YEAR! The employee who has been selected this year epitomizes a strong work ethic. This individual is 150% focused...

Music starts. It's 99 Luftballoons. Irene is distracted by the music and starts looking around the room. Irene tries to continue her speech.

IRENE:

Due to having a strong work ethic, this individual has been promoted in their 7 years...but . . . Bob . . . what are you . . .?

Bob is now walking towards her with microphone in hand. He begins to sing the beginning slow part of song, lovingly to Irene. Irene is confused and looks and feels awkward as he sings.

The song kicks in. Bob starts encouraging audience to clap hands. He is telling Irene to sing with him. When lyrics start up again She reluctantly sings to appease him hoping he will stop and move on. Bob continues singing. There is a choreographed slow melting of IRENE's cold exterior as she gets more and more into singing the song. Looking lovingly into her husbands eyes until there is full blown commitment and dance at the "power" moment of the song. Irenes hair comes down, literally, and she is "feeling" the song.

Bob during song is yelling out dance moves to patrons and employees. I.E. "Running Man" or "Water Sprinkler". The characters do whatever Bob tells them to do during song, characters encourage patrons to join them.

Irene sings song while everybody dances.

End of song, slow part, she turns and looks in Bobs eyes and sings the final slow verse IN GERMAN, and Irene and Bob kiss on final lyric..

While this final moment is happening all the employees have been handed red balloons by Kelly, with their backs to the audience, blow them up, concealing the now blown up balloons and then on the kiss raise them up and let them go as the balloons fly around the room.

EMPLOYEE OF THE YEAR
A WINNER-TAKE-ALL OFFICE PARTY SMACKDOWN

IRENE:
I am ALIVE! DANKESCHON! I love ALL OF YOU! I am going to learn all of your names!

She is handed a drink out of nowhere

This is my very first drink! Not tonight, ever! Ever!

Takes sip

OOOH what is that? vodka and Airborne? I like you all so much now. Seriously. I don't know where this microphone has been! Look! *(rubs it on her face; almost gags)* Look what I did! Okay is everybody ready?

Now the voting results for the EMPLOYEE OF THE

YEAR AWARD!!

IRENE:

Our Winner is _____________!!! Congratulations!

Cast runs on stage to congratulate winner

Gary:

Runs down to dancefloor waving camera

Let's get a picture!

Everybody poses – and yells out "OSHIOS". Gary takes picture

Lights go down - and a montage of photos that Gary has been taking all night come up on screen with Green Day's "Time of Your Life" playing. In the dark, the cast leaves the stage and heads to dressing room.

Gary:

On Mic Have a great night everybody! Thank you for coming.

Lights come up. Cast leaves room waving.

THE END

Extended Character Bios -

The "Non-Management" Employees

Lonnie Anderson

Lonnie is the warehouse manager from the local branch of OSHIOS. As a part of the outreach that OSHIOS is doing he has been selected to represent the branch and all of the dock-workers. He is a large gregarious man in his early to mid 40's with a big mouth and a larger heart. A former athlete he saw his dreams of football glory destroyed in the last play of his last high school game. He lost his full scholarship and began working in the loading dock. He has climbed the blue collar management ladder and is happy with his position. He is married with 2 kids but due to company policy his wife was not invited to attend this evenings event..

Ken Carrington

Ken was once the shining jewel in the Oshios crown. He started in the OSHIOS junior management training program...a fancy title that means intern. He worked his way up the ladder and vaulted over several other junior executives into a lower level senior management position. All the while on his climb up the ladder Ken was alienating people and destroying relationships. With

EMPLOYEE OF THE YEAR
WWW.EMPLOYEEOFTHEYEAR.ORG

nobody allies, friends or support in the company, he was terminated during a recent downsizing earlier this month. Because Monica Monica was so far into the planning stages of the party Ken has still been left on the list of invitees and was also left in the running for employee of the year. He shows up to the event, Uninvited, drunk and bitter and is almost single handedly ruining Monicas first ever event.

Shay Van Porquet

The sole representative for Employee of the year for all international

employees. Shay has never been to the U.S. before nor has he ever been out of his native country, “Shakenstienvia”. The only real contact he has had with any of these folks is with Ed Bunker, who has made consistent trips to Europe to train and hire staff. Shay’s job is to “run” the OSHIOS office in his native country. A job that seems to be faxing out daily reports, cleaning the office, and waiting for instructions on what he should do. Instructions that never seem to come.

Shay saw a picture of Ed’s daughter in his wallet and Shay contacted his daughter, Emily, and the two became engaged via email, much to the dismay and chagrin of Ed. Ed is beside himself that this has happened. Ed is aware that Shays intentions are about U.S. Citizenship and not about love. Shay loves the ladies and is a relentless flirt. His flirting and dancing with women throughout the evening infuriates Ed, as Shay is engaged to his daughter.

Sherman Allen

As the IT representative for the whole company Sherman was elected by his peers (when he was out sick one day) to represent the whole of the IT department as a canidate for Employee of the Year at this years event. Sherman gladly accepted the invitation, assuming that the party would be held at it's usual exotic locale, and he is slightly disappointed at this "scaled down"version of the event. Awkward and shy Sherman created the Video that is used at the events opening. When he first started at Oshios those many years ago, he was toured around the expansive Oshio's complex by , then HR intern, Dee Dee Blue. He has carried a torch for her ever since. This is his first time spending time with here in a social setting, since she was promoted to upper level management. However Dee Dee has her eyes set on Gary Kzerltkzerkzon.

EMPLOYEE OF THE YEAR
A WINNER-TAKE-ALL OFFICE PARTY SMACKDOWN
WWW.EMPLOYEEOFTHEYEAR.ORG

"The Management"

Gary Kzerltkzerkzon (pronounced "Shitserson")

Acquisitions Manager. His job aquire properties, business and other holdings for Oshios. He will work the room in pre-show asking people where they work and making a list of patrons employment and later in the show will announce recent acquisitions of OSHIOS which will be the companies that patrons have told him they work for. He will also be taking pictures throughout the evening. With about a half hour left in show all photo's Gary has taken will be downloaded by the Stage Manager so that a Ken Burns montage of all the photo's can play at the end of show.

Gary is straight laced, friendly and decent, in contrast to his job, which is to acquire and take over companies for OSHIOS. His job requires him to be cruel and show no mercy. But Gary himself is very likeable.

Gary spends the night avoiding the advances of Dee Dee Blue, whose advances become more and more direct as the night progresses and she has more to drink. The advances make Gary very awkward.

Monica Monica

A former NCAA division III Cheerleader champion Monica Monica has recently come to Oshios from a mildly successful event planning business.
After realizing the professional cheerleaders make no money and a couple of hazy months that

she spent making " independent art films" in the LA area Monica found her niche in events planning and client relations. After a brief, yet disasterous , turn in Bernie

Madoff's investor relations department Monica found it hard to find work. Then one day in a stipperobic's class she met Bob Clara Ingebertson Olson who introduced her to his

wife and the rest is history. This is here first large company event and, to make things even more difficult, she has been tasked with keeping the event positive and smooth over

any ruffled feathers that the new (more accessible...see

also lower budget) event has caused. She spends the night trying to “reel in” Ken Carrington, who in her mind is single handedly ruining everything, even though it’s her fault he was invited.

Ed Bunker

Vice President of Sales. 45 or older. He hates his job. But not as much as he hates Shay, who is engaged to his Daughter, (See Shay’s bio). Ed is cranky and surly.

Dee Dee Blue

Human Resources Director but is NOT very HR like. She has reputation for sleeping around. But is not obvious about it, things just “slip” out. Lot's of double-entendre stuff. Her outward demeanor is very HR, but says ordinary things that come off as sexual innuendo with her tone and body language. A simple “meet me in my office” has overtones of amore. She does an HR speech at top of show intended to establish not only her character and the rules for the office party but also to inform the audience of the boundaries with humor.

EMPLOYEE OF THE YEAR

“The rest of the characters”

Wanda Lamberton

Karaoke Host - the entertainment for the evening for the office Party. If the production is serving dinner, Wanda will start singing during dinner portion. She will be in a nice dress and be singing dinner music during the diner portion. She will do a costume change when it’s time for Karaoke/Dancing and change into her heavy metal, Blue collar garb.Heavy metal t-shirt, frizzed hair, etc. Wanda is from a small town. The town she is from should be a local joke.

Albert Lee Lamberton

Wanda's Husband and Roadie. He will run Karaoke machine and take patrons slips for song requests and sing a few songs himself. He also will be dressed well for the dinner segment and change clothes to his normal blue collar small town self for the Karaoke / dance segment.

Irene Clara Ingebretson-Olson - Shanan Custer

Company CEO - uptight, in charge and somewhat humorless. She is socially awkward, not a "bitch". She just does not like talking to people much. She is VERY uncomfortable talking to her employees. In fact she only sees them this one time a year. She will do a PowerPoint presentation at the beginning of the show. She loosens up at the end of the show when she is enticed by her husband to join him in a dance song number and we watch them fall in love again. Super afraid of germs.

Bob Clara Ingebretson-Olson

Irene's Husband, he took HER whole name when they got married. He is immasculated. He is very very happy and excited and just really fun, much to the dismay of his wife who is always trying to calm him down and get him to be serious. He has a great time dancing and talking with people all night. He gets her to loosen up at the end and realize why she fell in love with him in the first

---

place. Irene and Bob will sing "99 Luftballoons" to each other. Bob and Irene met in Germany and Bob is German.

Interns

These are extra cast members who will take on duties that are needed throughout the show. Cleaning, picking up "Employee of the Year" ballots, and any other show flow tasks that are needed. They are also understudies to regular cast members. They should have big "INTERN" nametags. It is up to the discretion of the production for how many interns they need and what there exact duties will be.

Kelly Phobo

Personal Assistant to Irene. Irene sends her to do tasks frequently throughout show. CEO is a germaphobe so part of Kelly's job is to make sure things stay clean. She is caught in the middle of the management types and the non- management types, and straddles the fence, since her job is very non- management but works directly with management. She is also uptight and very organized and calculating. Very efficient and very good at her job of taking care of Irene, and dresses very conservatively.

Tech Notes:

For the first year this is mandatory for producing companies of *Employee of the Year:*

EMPLOYEE OF THE YEAR
A WINNER-TAKE-ALL OFFICE PARTY SMACKDOWN
WWW.EMPLOYEEOFTHEYEAR.ORG

As a license of the show Employee of the Year you will receive the Oshios Logo and material needed for the reproduction of that Logo for Merchandise and Show related materials.

You will receive a branded template for the certificates

You will also receive a template for the EOY personal videos and the EOY voting updates

You will receive the opening Video for the show as well
You will receive the power point for Irene's speech

Tech Needs:

Projector and Screen Projector must have DVI or VGA input Karaoke Machine and sound system 2 Separate Mics for presentations Minimum 10' X 10" dance floor Minimum 14' X 8" staging Simple Lighting for Dance floor and lighting for Stage and presentations

Props

Award Certificates Employee of the Year
Trophy Various Business Cards Personal Props to be determined based on Character development

Important Notes if Dinner Is Included: It is imperative to the flow and pacing of the show that producers and directors work very closely with the caterers. It is very important that the food never become a joke in the production. Dinner must be served buffet style and it is very important to keep people moving so that dinner can be wrapping up by the time the "dinner music" section is finished.

Suggested Floor Plan:

Gray: Stage (see rider for minimum dimensions) Green: Dance Floor (see rider for minimum dimensions) Pink: Projector Red: Karaoke Set Up Blue: Presentation Area (see tech rider for minimum requirements)

Suggested Room Layout:

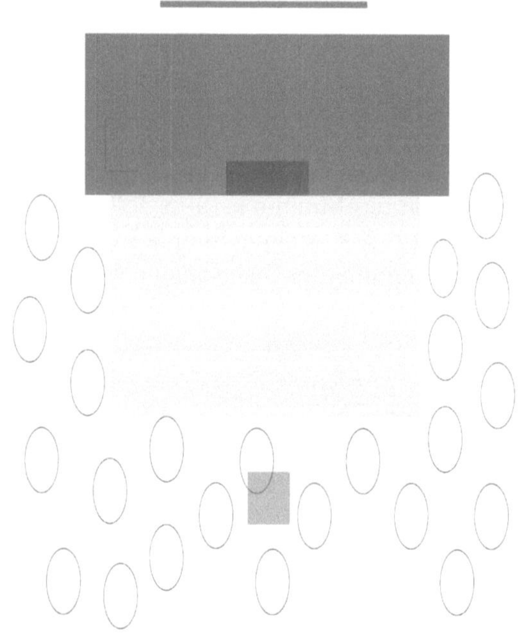

www.ingramcontent.com/pod-product-compliance
Ingram Content Group UK Ltd.
Pitfield, Milton Keynes, MK11 3LW, UK
UKHW041836200726
13854UKWH00003BA/1164

9 781105 528729